The Story

Beachy

L i g h t h o u s e

The light from the Beachy Head Lighthouse first shone on the 2nd October 1902.

Since that time it has stood heroically at the foot of Beachy Head, braved severe weather, withstood cliff falls and warned mariners of the dangers of this shore. It has been a temporary home for the keepers, survived a near miss with a mine during the Second World War and has operated independently since automation in 1982.

This is the story of the Beachy Head Lighthouse.

by Rob Wassell

RAW
Publications

1

The Story of the
Beachy Head
L i g h t h o u s e

Published by RAW Publications
www.rawpublications.co.uk

First printed March 2012
Reprinted March 2017

International Standard Book Number
ISBN 978-0-9569912-1-8

RAW
Publications
www.rawpublications.co.uk

The Beachy Head Lighthouse
'Trinitas in Unitate', Latin for 'Three in One'.
The Holy Trinity from where Trinity House took its name in 1514.

The chalk boulder strewn beach at Beachy Head

The White Chalk Cliffs

The white chalk cliffs at Beachy Head were formed between 65 and 100 million years ago when the land was completely covered by a warm sea.

They are the remains of coccoliths: plankton, that died and sank to the bottom. Compressed over time, they now form the dense, yet porous, rock that covers much of the South East of England.

The area between England and France was once a fertile low-lying tundra. At the end of the last Ice Age, approximately 10,000 years ago, the channel flooded with meltwater from the North Sea, thus forming the English Channel.

The pounding waves, wind, rain and icy winters take their toll on the fragile cliffs. Cracks become cavities which in turn become fissures which inevitably lead to a fall.

Sometimes there are exceptionally large falls, such as the one on 10th January 1999 when 6 metres of cliff fell over a length of 70 metres. The boulders form temporary barriers which help protect the cliff from the waves, until they wash away and the cycle begins again. This rate of erosion continues at an average of 60 centimetres per year.

Engraving of a shipwreck at Beachy Head, 1st July 1820

Two boys beneath Parson Darby's Hole in 1899

Wreck at Beachy Head

Dangerous Shores

The towering white cliffs at Beachy Head have long been a landmark for mariners. Yet a shelf of saw-like rock threatens danger to any vessel that comes too close to the shore. Having taken its toll of sailors' lives for centuries, Beachy Head remains a danger spot even today.

The government had been petitioned since 1691 to build a lighthouse at the top of the cliff, to provide a much needed warning for nearby ships.

In 1706, Jonathan Darby took up his role as Parson of the Parish of East Dean. He was deeply concerned at the number of drowned sailors, and especially so when an 800-ton schooner ran aground with the loss of all of her crew.

With his own hands, he dug out a series of tunnels in the cliff, including a cave 20 feet above the high water mark. It was from this cave that he shone a light which warned of the dangers of these treacherous waters.

He died on 26th October 1726 having saved many lives. His grave in East Dean churchyard reads: 'Here lies the body of Parson Darby. He was the sailors' friend.'

Shipwreck off Beachy Head

Shipwreck off Beachy Head

The First Lighthouse

When the East Indiaman, The Thames, became grounded and 'stuck fast' on the 3rd February 1822, the petition to erect a lighthouse gathered momentum. The Captain of the Royal Navy and Trinity House agreed to attend to the matter.

John 'Mad Jack' Fuller, MP for Sussex, witnessed the event himself and used his personal influence and some of his own wealth to fund the construction of the lighthouse.

In 1828, organised by Trinity House, a wooden lighthouse was erected at the cliff edge where lighting experiments were carried out.

The lighthouse proved to be a huge success and the number of shipwrecks was greatly reduced.

Parry's, 'The Coast of Sussex', published in 1833, refers to this early lighthouse:

'Further on, to the right, is the lighthouse on a projecting neck of land, capable of being seen at much greater distance by mariners when coming within distance of the shore. It has been erected of late years though seemingly called for long before.'

Lantern in place, late 1800s

Part-destroyed during World War 2

Moved in 1999, © BBC

Today, a luxury Bed and Breakfast

The Ill-fated Belle Tout

In 1832, work started on a permanent lighthouse.

On the 11th October 1834 the light first shone, yet its cliff-top location meant it was often obscured by mist and continual erosion threatened its future.

By the late 1800s the decision had been made to abandon Belle Tout and build a new lighthouse at the base of the cliffs.

In 1902 Belle Tout was decommissioned and sold to Mr Davies-Gilbert who ran it as a tea house.

In 1923 it was purchased by Sir James Purves-Stewart who remodelled it as a stately home.

Evacuated during the war, the lighthouse was used for gunnery practice by Canadian troops and left in ruins. Sir James was horrified and left the remains to Eastbourne Corporation.

Belle Tout was lovingly restored by the Cullinan family, used by the BBC to film 'The Life and Loves of a She-Devil' and moved 15 metres from the crumbling cliff edge by the Roberts family in 1999.

Rob Wassell's Trust tried to buy Belle Tout in 2007.

David and Barbara Shaw bought the building in 2008 and have turned it into a luxury B&B.

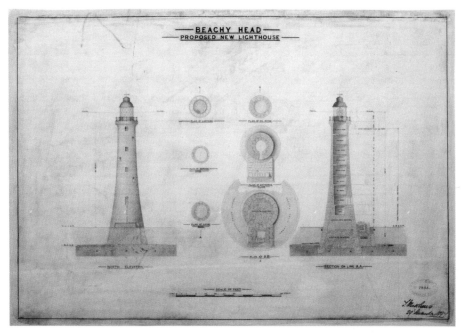

Sir Thomas Matthews' plans for the Beachy Head Lighthouse

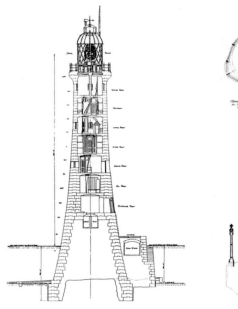

Cross section drawing

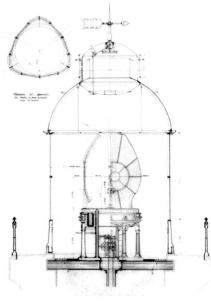

Douglass Helical Lantern and Optics

The New Lighthouse

In 1898, Sir Thomas Matthews, Trinity House's Engineer in Chief, began working on the plans and specifications for a new lighthouse at Beachy Head.

The chosen location was to be 700ft (213m) from the base of the chalk cliffs, one and a quarter miles to the east of Belle Tout.

A bore hole was initially dug to ensure that the new tower would be standing on a secure foundation.

Trinity House appointed Albert Havelock Case as resident engineer to oversee the project.

However, the project was posed with a unique problem - how to get the essential equipment and building materials to the proposed site, 530ft (131m) below the cliff.

With Cow Gap one and a quarter miles to the East, and Birling Gap two miles to the West, beach access was completely impractical.

In addition, there was the added obstacle of the high tides, twice a day, that could reach a height of almost 26ft (8m).

Mr Case came up with a rather ingenius solution.

The cable ropeway, Scientific American

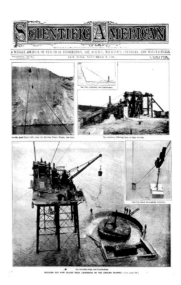

Scientific American, 1901

The foreshore platform, Scientific American, 9th November 1901

Challenging Construction

Extensive work was done at the top of the cliffs, including a road system, and railway lines to carry a large mobile 'Goliath' steam crane. Barracks were built to house the workforce of 53 men.

A cable ropeway was erected on the edge of the cliff, extending down 550ft (168m) to the construction platform that was built on the foreshore.

The materials to build the platform, which was mostly steel in construction, were delivered by steam ship. The platform was anchored to the chalk sea bed using concrete stanchions and rose to 23ft (7m) above the high water mark.

A coffer dam was erected for the safety of the men working on the site and to provide protection for the foundations of the lighthouse during these early stages of construction.

Iron sheets were hammered into the soft upper layer of chalk to a height of 8ft (2.5m) above high water. Concrete was used to finish the dam.

The site was 50ft (15m) in diameter and included a tidal sluice and steam-powered pumps, which ran continuously to drain the dam after each high tide.

'The illustration shows the aerial ropeway from the works to the top of Beachy Head'

'The works and a flowing tide'

The Black and White Budget

In The Headlines

The Black and White Budget from the 30th March 1901 features the progress of the new lighthouse:

'The building of the new lighthouse at famous Beachy Head is proceeding apace. The Belle Tout lighthouse has been voted rather ancient, and consequently another beacon is to be erected. The difficulties are great, but our photos show that the foundations have already been laid. As that is the worst part, the tower itself will soon make its welcome appearance.'.

The Scientific American from the 9th November 1901 has an extensive article written by Harold J Shepston of London, England:

'The new lighthouse which the Corporation of Trinity House are erecting off Beachy Head, on the English south coast, is an interesting piece of work on account of the scientific manner in which it is being carried out. '

'The coast was thoroughly surveyed and at last a site was chosen. Curiously enough, a large steamer was wrecked not many months ago on the very same spot selected and became a total wreck.'

Men being lowered in a large bucket

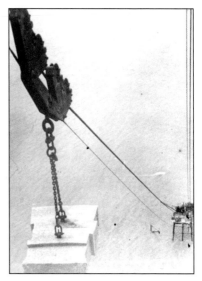

A dovetail block being lowered

860ft from cliff to lighthouse

The cable ropeway hoisting gear at the top of the cliff, Scientific American 1901

'The site is some 550 feet from the top of the cliffs and at high tide is covered to considerable depth. This makes the work doubly interesting, for there is a wonderful difference between erecting a structure on a wave-washed rock and on land.'

'There are two fixed ropes, stretched parallel between the two points, 860 feet apart. One has a circumference of 6 inches and the other 5½ inches. The former has a breaking strain of 120 tons, and the latter 100 tons. These ropes terminate at a massive wooden trestle erected in the workyard on the cliff tops.'

'This unique ropeway has now been working efficiently for some twelve months. It is used every day, and during the early stages of the work often at night. Some heavy pieces of machinery, such as pumps, a steam engine, crane, etc., as well as large quantities of cement, shingle etc., have been safely sent down to the temporary landing stage. The stones, the heaviest loads, always descend on the 6-inch rope, and on the parallel rope a balance load is run which the stones descending draw up, thus considerably reducing the necessary brake power.'

Quarrymen of the De Lank Quarry, St. Brewards, nr Bodmin, Cornwall, circa 1900

The numbered granite blocks, Scientific American, 9th November 1901

Cornish Granite

Used with great success in the Eddystone lighthouse and also Tower Bridge, Blackfriars Bridge and the Thames Embankment, it was decided to use Cornish granite from the De Lank quarries at St. Brewards near Bodmin in Cornwall.

Each granite block was shaped and prepared at the quarry to exact specifications using a wooden template. Most were 22in (55.9cm) thick with a dovetail to fit snugly against the next stone.

Each block was then matched with its partner to ensure a tight fit and then individually numbered.

The blocks, which weighed between one and two tons each, were then loaded on to railway wagons to begin their journey to Eastbourne station.

There are 26 courses of interlocking granite blocks, the joints between them filled with cement. 'Thus making the tower as firm as if it were in one solid piece' reports the Scientific American.

The tower is a height of 141ft (43m) and includes approximately 50,000 cubic feet of granite and 1,300 cubic yards of concrete hearting.

The total weight of granite used was 3,660 tons.

Construction proceeding well, the oil room level, just above the entrance, 1901

Over halfway

Nearly finished, 1902

The Structure of the Lighthouse

The front door is accessible via a ladder which leads into the main lobby. The toilet is on this floor with a 1,600 gallon water tank below.

The very steep staircase leads to the station's oil supply and pressurised paraffin tanks.

On the next level is the crane room with a manually-operated hoist used to lift supplies. This would also have served as a storage room.

The main storage area was on the floor above.

The living quarters were on the next level, which included a cast-iron cooking range within a solid granite surround. It was cleaned every day.

The bedrooms above consisted of five beds, known as 'banana bunks' as they were shaped to fit the contours of the wall. Each bunk had its own wardrobe, chest of drawers and privacy curtain.

The watch room housed a large cast-iron stanchion to support the weight of the optical apparatus in the lantern room above. It also had a table, chairs, a curved wooden bookcase and cupboards.

The walls are 9ft (2.7m) at the thickest point and taper in thickness as they rise towards the top.

Various photographs restored from original glass plates taken by Alfred George May

The Last Stone

On the 25th February 1902 the last stone was laid.

At 17:00 on the 2nd October 1902, the Beachy Head Lighthouse was lit for the first time. It flashed twice every 20 seconds with a range of 16 miles.

The light assembly weighed just over 4 tons and floated in an annular tray containing about 900lbs (408kg) of mercury. A weight on a steel wire dropped down a tube to make the optic turn and required rewinding every four hours.

Black stripes were painted to help the tower stand out from the white chalk background, the light granite blocks themselves almost appearing white.

The whole project was finished six weeks early and around £4,490 lower than expected with a total cost of £56,000 - around £4.7 million by comparison with prices in 2010.

The maximum number of men working at any one time was 53 and the average number 28. The weekly wage per man during the contract came to £1.11s.8d - equivalent to £538 a week. The salary of a long-service Principal Keeper was £70 per year - equivalent to around £24,000.

The Beachy Head Lighthouse and Cliffs, postcard dated 15th April 1907

Beachy Head, 1947, © Aero Pictorial Ltd

The War Years

During the First World War, many ships were sunk by German submarines that hid in the depths of the Channel. The light at Beachy Head was lit throughout the war, but only at half-power, by order of the Admiralty, to aid passing allied convoys.

During World War II the light was only lit when requested to help damaged aircraft find their way back home. It could take up to fifteen minutes to fire-up the lamp so instead the keepers came up with the solution of using a kitchen lamp. "The rays were much narrower but the light served its purpose", recalls Reginald Simon, Principal Keeper.

The keepers also had a rather tense moment when they observed a mine drifting towards the lighthouse. 'We passed the word to the naval authorities and were told that if it was over 200 yards away to attempt to sink it by gunfire. We told whoever it was at the other end that we had no guns, and after a slight hesitation he said, "Well, just standby". It continued to drift towards us and in a few minutes it passed with no more than three feet to spare, heading for the shore where it struck a rock and exploded, blackening the cliff to the very top.'

Bob Collis, pumping tanks, 1948 © ALK   Santa Claus visits, 1948 © ALK

Bob Collis, 23, trainee, one week on the job, cooking a meal, 1948 © ALK

Life as a Lighthouse Keeper

Mark Hunter was offered the position of Supernumary Lighthouse Keeper on 2nd September 1974.

'It has been decided to send you to Beachy Head Lighthouse to undergo some training at this station before attending the Training School. You should travel early on Monday, 9th September 1974, to Eastbourne, Sussex, and, on your arrival, telephone the Lighthouse at Eastbourne 24839. Mr Gauld, the Principal Keeper, will advise you about ordering your stores and how to get to the Lighthouse. The relief at Beachy Head is done overland according to the state of the tides. Bedding and blankets will be available for you at the Lighthouse, and you should take some old clothes for working in.'

Mark was to have the 'luxury' of being taken to the lighthouse by boat, rather than walk the rock-strewn beach beneath the crumbling chalk cliffs.

"Mr Neville Dean was exactly what you might expect of a local fisherman, beard, wellingtons, naval cap and a healthy disdain for landlubbers."

"It was a thrilling moment when we came round the bottom of the cliffs and I saw the tower for the first time from sea level."

Bill James, Dick Packer and John Dobinson playing cribbage, c1950s, © ALK

John Dobinson and Dick Packer reading the news in the kitchen, c1950s, © ALK

"The first thing we all did after the boat had disap-peared from sight was to sit down and have a cup of tea. This may sound simple enough but I soon found out that it was not simply a matter of switch-ing on an electric kettle – there was no electric! At that time the lighthouse was not on the mains electric supply and all that there was in the way of electrical goods was a few car batteries rigged up to a wind generator on the lantern gallery. This arrangement, provided there was enough wind to power the generator, gave enough power for three lights, portable television and an alarm for the main light."

"I did not realise at the time that Beachy Head was almost unique in being so unmodernised and I was so lucky to see a lighthouse almost in its original working order. Every other rock tower would have had by then at least a diesel engine and generator to power, if not the main light, at least the domestic services."

"The tower was very quiet. You would hear boats approaching or changes in the wind more easily. The downside was that when you were on watch at night and the others were in bed, you were always aware that any noise would be easily heard."

Attaching Tonite charge, 1948, © ALK

Cleaning the lantern, undated, © ALK

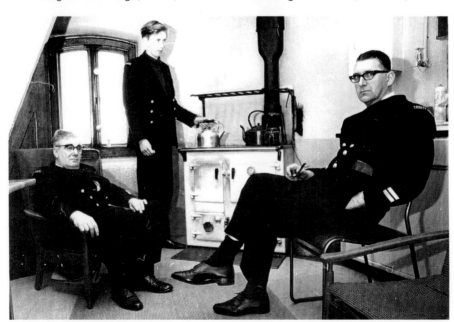

Gordon Harthill (Right) with his two colleagues in the Kitchen, undated, © ALK

"There were three keepers and somebody had to be 'on watch', i.e. responsible, every hour of the day. The answer was to work two days of twelve hours and get twenty-four hours free of duty."

Each day started at 4am and Mark would work from 4am-12pm and 8pm-12am on the first day, 12pm-8pm and 12am-4am on the second day. However, "When you are on a lighthouse you can do nothing very productive with a day off!"

"The tidal effect was another reason why Beachy Head was unique among tower lighthouses and was a great boon in giving the keepers a chance, at least for an hour or two, to stretch the legs on walks along the foreshore. It also gave us the chance to catch crabs, lobsters and prawns which supplemented our diet and were so fresh that I haven't tasted better ones since."

"Although Beachy Head was behind other tower lights, it did have a (sea water) flush toilet. Other towers had to make do with the original camping-style commonly called the 'bucket and chuck it'. The only drawback was that in very rough seas it did occasionally lose its non-return flap on the waste pipe with the consequent rush of sea water up the pipe which could be quite disconcerting."

Gordon Harthill cleaning the lens, undated, © ALK

Relief day, c1950s © ALK   Weather report journals, c1950s © ALK

In 1951 it was decided to make the lighthouse more distinctive and this was to be achieved by re-painting the black stripes red. It wasn't until 1980 that it was re-painted red and white to help visibility of the lighthouse from a greater distance. "During fog we detonated Tonite charges to warn shipping. They were 4oz sticks of explosive, similar to dynamite. They were detonated every 5 minutes. We didn't get much sleep those nights." Recalls Ted Frostick, while stationed there in 1974.

Dai Woosnam was 22 when he served at Beachy Head. "I will never forget it. Gordon was in his quarters resting when we heard his quiet painful cries for help. We found him gripping his chest from a heart attack." Dai called the Coastguard.

"The biggest problem was getting Gordon down to the boat. He was about 16 stone and there was no way he could be brought down the incredibly tight spiral staircase." They tied Gordon to a stretcher and lowered him down through the top window.

"Handing me the other end of the rope I started to be dragged up the side - fortunately, a burly life-boatman managed to grab the last remaining few inches of my rope and stop the fiasco."

Gordon Harthill made a full recovery.

Entrance © Koellner '93

Stairs © Koellner '93

Engine Room © Koellner '93

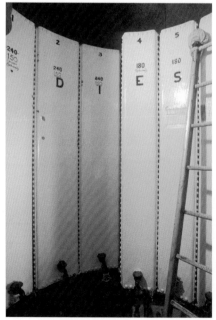

Tanks © Koellner '93

Electrification

In 1975, the lighthouse switched over to electricity using a new 'first order catadioptic' apparatus with a 400 watt bulb. Flashing twice every 20 seconds, the light could be seen up to 27 nautical miles away. This marked the end of 72 years of oil power The lack of space inside the tower was the main reason that it hadn't been electrified until then.

An electricity cable was laid across the headland providing power from the top of the cliff. Large red plastic balls were attached to the cables to warn low-flying planes of the dangers of flying between the lighthouse and the cliff, as had happened previously severing the telephone lines.

A diesel generator was installed which would start automatically in the event of power failure. A three-wick Douglass oil lamp could also be fitted by the keepers in case of complete power failure.

No longer did the keepers need to pump oil during their watch and the lack of fumes made life considerably more comfortable. The smell of paraffin had its unlikely benefits though, according to one keeper, it was nearly always possible to obtain a compartment to themselves on the train home.

Bedroom © Koellner '93

Kitchen © Koellner '93

Automation

In 1981, Trinity House began automating the Beachy Head Lighthouse, which would be monitored from the Trinity House Operations and Planning Centre in Harwich, Essex.

Telemetry equipment was installed, together with a back-up generator and an atmospheric detector which would measure air pressure and detect visibility between its sensors. When required, it would operate the 2000 watt 'nautophone' fog signal.

When news of automation was announced, objections were raised by the Coastguard, Cliff Rescue and the police. The keepers were in the ideal position to sound the alarm when people fell, or walkers got stranded or ships ran aground.

'Their help has really been invaluable. Nothing can replace their co-operation and help and quite honestly I hope these changes never happen', said Gary Russell, Chief Coastguard, Gazette, 1981.

On the 28th June 1983 the lighthouse was switched over to automatic operation and the keepers who were on duty, Tony Beswetherick, Jim Lossie and Mike Hall, left for the very last time.

Saving the Stripes

In June 2010, Trinity House, as part of their Aids to Navigation Review, announced that they would be reducing the range of the light to eight nautical miles and the fog horn would be discontinued.

Trinity House also decided that the lighthouse was no longer required to act as a 'daymark' and further costs would be saved by not painting the lighthouse and letting it fade to its original grey colour.

The Save the Stripes campaign was launched on 14th October 2011 to help raise money to repaint the lighthouse and restore this iconic landmark to its former glory. A Facebook group was set up and progress was followed closely by Eastbourne Herald and the nation's media - support quickly grew.

The re-painting cost was £45,000, to be part-funded by Trinity House. £27,000 was the fundraising target of the campaign. Hempel Crown and Brewers donated the paint.

Eastbourne AM Rotary Club organised a walk to the lighthouse. There was a competition to see the lighthouse up close by boat and even this very book was written to help raise money for the repainting of the stripes.

Michael Fish, Neil Oliver, John Craven, Griff Rhys-Jones, Bill Bryson and Eddie Izzard, who grew up in Bexhill and went to school in Eastbourne, were just some of the famous names helping the cause. Donations were coming in fast, including £1,000 from the Duke of Devonshire and a very generous £10,000 from Eastbourne Borough Council.

The big break came on 21st October 2012 when the campaign appeared on Countryfile. By the 5th November the fundraising target had been met.

Sussex Blast Cleaning won the contract. Following paint specification sign-off and a delay due to bad weather, the work began on 20th September 2013. A team of abseilers pressure-washed the lighthouse, applied the primer and then painted five coats of paint onto the lantern and three coats of red and white stripes on the tower using rollers.

On the 8th October the Save the Stripes team and BBC Breakfast News visited the lighthouse.

Work was completed on the 10th October and used 6,000 litres of water for the pressure washer, 2,000 litres of water for drinking and washing and 700 litres of red and white paint to cover approximately 800m2 of granite and 300m2 of mixed iron work. The paint is rated to last for ten years.

Quadrophenia, 1979

Chitty Chitty Bang Bang, 1968

The Chalk Garden, 1964

The Prisoner, 1968

Beachy Head in Film

The area of Beachy Head and Eastbourne has been a popular film location in some notable movies:

Brighton Rock, 2010
Notes on a Scandal, 2006
Harry Potter & the Goblet of Fire, 2005
Wimbledon, 2004
Band of Brothers, 2001
Pearl Harbour, 2001
Last Orders, 2001
Tom and Viv, 1994
Robin Hood Prince of Thieves, 1991
The Krays, 1990
James Bond: The Living Daylights, 1987
Tommy, 1975
Half a Sixpence, 1967

...and many more, including made-for-TV programmes such as Foyles War and Miss Marple.

The Beachy Head Lighthouse itself makes an appearance in The Chalk Garden, Quadrophenia, Chitty Chitty Bang Bang and an episode of the Prisoner from 21st January 1968, called 'The Girl Who Was Death'. At the end of the episode, the lighthouse blows up in spectacular fashion.

Beachy Head is a very special place for me. It's magical, spectacular, breath-taking, wild and natural and the Beachy Head Lighthouse with its iconic red and white stripes has become as much part of Beachy Head as the white cliffs themselves.

In 2007 I tried to buy the nearby Belle Tout Lighthouse by public subscription and you can find out more about the history of this fascinating building in my book, 'The Story of the Belle Tout Lighthouse' ISBN 978-0-9569912-0-1. I am delighted to still be involved with Belle Tout.

Thank you to Heather for her love and unending support and Tina and Marc for their friendship and eagle-eyed proof-reading skills.

Rob Wassell
rob@beachyheadlighthouse.co.uk

Visit www.beachyheadlighthouse.co.uk for more information about the Beachy Head Lighthouse and the Save the Stripes campaign.

All photography, writing and content by Rob Wassell unless otherwise credited.

Many of the old photographs and postcards I have acquired over the years and some of their origins are unknown. My apologies If I have failed to give credit, I have not done so on purpose and will gladly correct this in future if brought to my attention.

Thank you to Sheila Ryan, a fellow writer, who very kindly provided me with such incredible background information on lighthouse keepers. http://www.sheila-ryan.com

Thank you to Kath Clarke for the use of her Grandfather, Alfred George May's amazing photos taken during the construction process on page 24

Thank you also to Andreas and Claudia Koellner for a unique glimpse into the inside of the lighthouse from 1993 on page 36 and 38. http://www.eu-faro.de

Page 12, 18 plans, drawings and old pictures, copyright Trinity House

Page 14, 18, 20, the Scientific American, 9th November 1901

Page 16, the Black and White Budget, 30th March 1901

Page 20, the De Lank Quarrymen, http://jackiefreemanphotography.com/st_breward.3.htm

Page 22, copyright Trinity House, R Brutnell and Central Eastbourne Library

Page 28, 30, 32, 34, copyright the Association of Lighthouse Keepers. http://www.alk.org.uk

Page 44, copyright of the respective production companies

Reference material: Beachy Head by Martin Boyle, Beachy Head by John Surtees